Fundamentals of Sprinting

Fundamentals of Sprinting

"A Guide for High School Sprinters"

####
The more knowledge that you know as a coach the better
you can prepare your athlete for Success!

Eugene Shane Lee
and Jeremiah Whitfield

"The E. Shane Lee Company, Inc." © 2009

To order additional copies of this book, contact:
Xlibris Corporation
1-888-795-4274
www.Xlibris.com
Orders@Xlibris.com
70609

Table of Contents

ACKNOWLEDGEMENTS

I N WRITING THIS book there have been some individuals that we have watched and learned from over the years. These individuals have given us words of encouragement and they have helped us learn to develop our own Track & Field philosophy. These mentors are:

- Grantis Bell – Head Lady's Coach of Fort Lauderdale High
- David Martin – Head Boy's Coach of Fort Lauderdale High
- David Shepherd – Track & Field Coach of St. Thomas High

We also want to give a special thanks to the coaching staff that we worked with while writing this book. We have all helped each other grow as coaches. These coaches are:

- John Battle – Head Boy's Coach of Hallandale High
- Frank Hammond – Asst. Coach of Hallandale High
- Albert Guzzo – Athletic Director of Hallandale High
- Frederica Carter – Asst. Athletic Director of Hallandale High

To the best group of athletes that anyone could ever coach: The Hallandale Men's & Lady's Track and Field Team. These are a group of runners that work very hard and are very serious about wanting to be the best. We also want to mention and give thanks to: Brittany, Dawn, Dominique, Elise, Erica, India, Jasmine, Jeneil, Keyva, Makdalaine, Monique, Natresha, Rose, Sasha, Shekia, Tashaunda, Taqauyla, Toraya, and Tracey. They are the greatest group of young ladies to be blessed to know and coach.

To our motivators that keep us on our toes whether it is in coaching or in conversation. They make sure we present the best training method to the ladies. Thanks to Kyri Tabor, LaShae Sherrell, and Natasia Kennedy.

We also thank Mrs. Fran Carter-West for her support and standing by us everywhere we go.

Thank you to Antoinette Foreman for being our model runner in the photos.

And I give Special Thanks to: Tolanda Ingram, Anita Edwards, Ashley Dukes, and Sallie Green thanks for your approval.

This book is dedicated to all of you! Thanks for all of your support.

PREFACE

T HIS IS THE first edition of the series *Fundamentals of Sprinting*. You will find that the goal of the first series will offer high school coaches and athletes basic instructions on sprint techniques, sprint training, sprint starts, and sprint finishes.

Most books are written for the professional and college athlete causing you to water down techniques and training tips to fit it into the short high school season. However, this book is not written for those elite athletes and coaches, it is directed to those individuals who find it difficult to teach to those unknown about sprinting. This book is meant to help form high school athletes into elite athletes.

We believe that the high school level is the most important level in shaping an individual athlete for the future. During this time you are able to find out whether or not the athlete can participate on the next level. If the coach is able to teach and train the athlete on a fast paced level it makes it easier for them to make a transition to the next level.

Fundamentals of Sprinting Book Series will concentrate on teaching:

○ Progressions/ Workouts – Events 100, 200, and 400 meters
○ Block Starts and Block Drills
○ Drills – Sprint Drills, Acceleration Drills, etc.
○ Weight Training – Upper Body, Lower Body, and Safety
○ Core work
○ Flexibility training
○ Plyometrics

As coaches this book will allow you to gain a wealth of information in order to teach and train athletes to have a great and successful season. You will give your young athlete access to learn and improve their work ethics. This series will help you breakdown the way you coach certain events, and it will help you understand how to utilize workouts to help you reach your full potential.

INTRODUCTION

A S A COACH the first task to complete is to evaluate the sprinters to know what level they are on for training proposes. Plan to have an organized scheduled for the week, month, or the year. Make short term and long term goals; make sure that the goals are very reachable for the athlete being trained. There are some questions that you must ask in the planning process:

1. How do I identify the sprinters?
2. Are the athletes able to catch on to the fast paced workouts?
3. Are the athletes mentally prepared to run the sprints?
4. Can the athlete handle the physical workouts to become better?
5. What type of workouts should I do on a daily basis?

Those are some questions that one must be able to think about and ask to oneself. The coach wants to be able to identify who the sprinters are early so that no time is wasted in training someone in an area where they are not comfortable (especially if it is seen that they are not going to benefit themselves or the team in that area). So, in the decision making process, be aware and careful because a lot of high school runners think that they're fast, but as a coach it can be seen early the individuals that fit the mode of a sprinter.

There are key elements that a coach wants to cover in the development of a sprinter and this book will cover most of everything that is needed to learn and teach. This will help in the preparation in teaching techniques, drills, form, etc. High School Track & Field is changing every year and athletes are adapting to the information on what is being taught faster and using the opportunity to become stronger and quicker. So the more they learn the better they become.

SPRINTS

S PRINT RACE CATEGORIES include all distances up to 400m, with the 400m being concluded as a long sprint. When looking at hurdling (from the 100m, 300m, 400m hurdles for the women and 110m, 300m, 400m hurdles for the men) most coaches would look upon those races as a form of sprinting with the clearance of jumping over the hurdles. The sprint races that we are going to be dealing with are 100m, 200m, and 400m. In this section we are going to cover sprint techniques, speed development, sprint start, and 100m training.

One of the most important keys to becoming a better sprinter is learning the proper technique of how to sprint while learning how to position the body to be able to run faster. When sprinting, the athlete runs on the balls of their feet with the upper body either in an upright or inclined position. Their arms are flexed at a 90 degree angle at the elbow with their face and hands relaxed and their legs extended into a powerful motion. The athlete should not raise their hips forward or backwards. The hips should stay in the same motion throughout the sprint. Your feet should be pointed forward never down.

When following this process, you will see the athlete begin to run faster. And in continuing this type of motion the athlete will get used to the proper form and mechanics in order to become a better and faster sprinter.

SPRINT DRILLS/SPRINT TECHNIQUES

O NE OF THE most important activities to make a sprinter better is warming up and cooling down. It actually improves the sprinters ability to learn accelerating and sprint endurance. It will also aid in the process of recovery needed before training begins and also competing again. Specific spring drills are used to correct posture and running motions. These drills will also aid in learning the appropriate range of motion the body should use while sprinting. ***Note: Sprint drills are to be done in running shoes or cross trainers, never done in spikes.***

General sprint drills or warm up routines are as follows:

1. A-walk

    •   Coordinated tall walk using your right arm with left leg and vice versa. Maintain a 90 degree angle with your elbow, knee, and ankle.

2. High knees

    •   Take a short stride bouncing on your toes, raise your knees to your chest, you will concentrate on the form or raising your knees. You will move in distance until the drill is finished.

3. A-skips

    - Skip using your right arm with the left leg and vice versa. Maintain a 90 degree angle with your elbow, knee, and vice versa.

4. B-skips

    - Do the A-Skip and add an extension of your upper leg before your leg hits the ground.

5. Side-steps/ Carioca

    - Move sideways at an upbeat pace. Your left foot is to cross in front of your right, your right foot steps right, your left foot is to cross behind your right, your right foot steps right, and you repeat those steps the opposite way. Remember body is in the upright position.

6. Backwards running

    - Normal running form backwards. You don't want to reach with your legs.

7. Walking lunges

    - You start with your feet 6 inches apart with your toes pointed forward. Step forward with your left leg and you lower your body to a 90 degree angle at both knees. Remember to put your weight on your heels. Repeat this same step with your right leg.

8. Heels and toes

    - While walking on your heels the toes must be pointed in the upright position using your arms in a 90 degree angle movement.
    - While walking on your toes you must be on the balls of your feet lifting your legs in an opposite motion of your arms.

9. Straight let (Run out)

    - Stand straight up placing either your right or left leg 6 inches in front of your body. You will bend over and reach to touch your toes. You will alternate legs.

10. Fast leg drills

- Running with quick knee lifts, once you lift you right leg you alternate to your left leg.

11. Accelerations

- Beginning with a slow jog increase your speed over a distance until finished. (example: 0m to 30m)

12. Butt Kicks

- Fast movement driving your knees up and bringing the heel under the buttock having your thighs parallel to the ground.

13. Quick Feet

- This is quick reaction drill taking baby steps with very fast leg action. Your arms and feet move very quickly, you must be on the balls of your feet.

These drills are designed to help the athlete warm up and focus on the mechanics of running. The athlete should always be relaxed and focused on becoming better at each drill. The drills are always led by the coach or by a designated leader of the track team to make sure that they are done properly. In order to see the difference in your training, the drills must be done right. All drills should be done over a 30 to 40 meter distance.

BLOCK START

BEFORE YOUR BODY runs in motion, before you have a chance to accelerate, before you can finish a race you have to start. The start is one of the most vital parts of completing any race. There are many different components that can be used to learn the proper technique for a great sprint start. The sprint start can be very technical and hard for those who have never tried it before. But with this book we are going to break it down so you as a coach or athlete can understand just how easy and comfortable learning the start can be. In this chapter we are going to cover:

- Block settings
- On your mark positions
- Set position
- When the gun sounds

We are going to cover block drills that you can do with the blocks or without the blocks and this is going to have you learn how to be comfortable in learning the proper technique. Also, we are going to talk about how you should establish a routine and stick with it every time you get in the blocks. And last in this chapter we will cover how to work on your reaction time. What type of drills you can do to make your reaction time better and faster. You want to remember that practice makes perfect, you want to get yourself adjusted and used to how the blocks feel and how to come out of them. Once this is perfected it will help you out a lot with speed development. The shorter the distance of the race the more the sprinter relies on their start. So, are you ready, well "On your marks . . . Get Set . . . Let's Go!"

Block Settings

It is very important to know how to set your blocks up at the starting line. The first thing you want to do is make sure that the fronts of your starting blocks are estimated about 1 foot behind the starting line. The athlete will take their foot and place their heel at the starting line and place the block at the tip of the toe. You can use this setup and it would allow you to start the same each time.

Foot Placement

Now you have to determine the difference between "Power Leg" and "Lead Leg." The leg that you kick a ball with or the leg that you jump the highest on is considered your power leg. So that leaves your opposite leg to be your Lead Leg. The distance from the start line is very important.

Power Leg – This would be the leg that is the closet to the starting line that gives you 100% of your forward movement. Setting the first pedal, you want to use a method that you could feel most comfortable in doing and that would allow you to start the best.

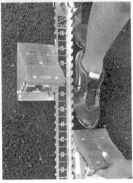

Lead Leg – This is your back leg which is the farthest from the starting line. Once you push off with your power leg this leg comes forward and it lands about 2-3 feet past the starting line. The distance is depending upon the way your foot is set on the blocks to get the push out for distance.

Remember the more you work the starting block the more comfortable you become in them and you will be able get a smoother rhythm. This is the simplest way that you could get a great routine for a good start.

"On your Marks"

Once you hear this call you know that it is time to get ready to get into your starting block. Your block should already be set before this call. You should be focused on the routine that you always use to get in your block. We recommend that you stand behind your block before you hear this call. Once the call is made you should walk out in front of your block get down and walk back into your blocks stretching your hamstrings and calves. You place your power leg on the front pedal and you place your lead on the back pedal. Remember the balls of your feet should be on the pedals and never your heels.

Your hands should be positioned behind the starting line about 1 inch outside of your shoulders with your fingers together. You will create a bridge with your fingers and thumb; fingers will be parallel to the starting line. Make sure your fingers never touch the starting line. You will drop your head, relax your shoulders, but never tense up. Remember to remain motionless when you get in position, any movement will result in a false start and a possible disqualification.

Set Position

Once you are down now it is time to get set. Once you are in the blocks and you hear "Set" your front leg which your power leg your knee is bent at 90 degrees. And your back leg, which is your lead leg, will be bent at between 125-130 degrees. At this time the only thing that should be on the track will be your thumbs and your forefingers.

It is very important that your hand is set an equal distance with your shoulders. Your shoulder will be slightly over your hands which will be parallel to the starting line. Your hips will be raised above your shoulders, remember to use more of your back leg to raise your hips.

At this time your head will be down, look downward at the track and you also want to relax your neck, and your shoulders. You want to think of how the mechanics of a pinball machine works, one you pull back the lever and the spring is in a recoil position when you let the lever go you have a mass explosion. That is the idea of this position is to be coiled tight for a great start. Remain still in this position also, if there is any movement is will result in a false start or disqualification.

Note: In the position of "On your marks" and "Set" if you do not feel right or you know something is wrong, at any time before the gun goes off you can raise your hand. When the starter recognizes you everyone can run out and you can start this process all over again so you can get it right.

Starter Gun Goes Off

First you want to think of your movement instead of thinking about the sound of the gun. That is the key to your concentration of getting out of the blocks. Remember to allow your body to drive out of the blocks then running up and out of the blocks. The body should come out at an angle and slowly rise up while running down the track. Push out with both feet driving the arm of the power leg side forward first, and then take a long and powerful stride out of the blocks. That step should be fast and powerful so you can have an effective start.

Reaction drills

There are many drills that you can use in practice that can get you comfortable in coming out of the blocks. You can get a coach or a fellow athlete that can call out the cadence and clap their hands together. On some days you could use a starters' pistol or a whistle. You can repeat these steps until you see results.

100 METERS

THE 100 METERS is a full sprint and is the shortest of the outdoor races. When in high school every athlete thinks of 100 meters as a glamour and exciting race that every athlete would love to have a chance to run. To run the 100 meters effectively you must use speed, power, flexibility, strength, great work ethic & most of all your brain. There is no time to think while running this race; you must be able to know how to manage this race before you step onto the track. You should be prepared and relaxed to do exactly what you were trained to do.

Phases of the 100 meters

As a runner you should understand the race and how it is broken down. There are many different philosophies that many use on the high school level. Some may work and some may keep you wondering. Many coaches will tell you that you must get a good start and run fast. Well we look at it in a different way, we believe that your start must be great, but if you can follow a method you will see your time decrease.

In coaching high school track and field we found out that if you have a plan on how to help the athlete manage their particular event, then you will see great results throughout the year. For the 100 meters you should break it down by phases, this will allow your athlete to learn the race and use the phases to know where they are on the track and what they have to do in order to be successful in the 100 meters. Keep in mind to introduce these phases to the athlete early around January. Therefore, when the season starts they will have full knowledge of how to run the 100 meters.

The phases are as follows:

- The Start
- Drive Phase: 0m-20m
- Acceleration (initial & full): 20m-45m
- Maximum Speed: 45m-60m
- Maintaing Speed: 60m-100m
- The Finish

The Start (7-10 Steps)

The first thing is to get your body moving in the right direction. In order to do that you must have a sound start. Some athletes are so impatient and want to quickly get in the starting blocks. Then start running and rely on their speed to keep them in the race. Typically, the athlete just wants to run, but we believe that starting correctly could lead to a great race. This is the most important phase of the 100 meters. This phase consist of 7 to 10 steps, the steps depends on the athletes height. In starting your body must not pop up; we will state again: "In starting your body must not pop up." This is very crucial because if the body pops up in this phase you will have a lot of trouble throughout the 100 meters. Applying the proper force to your start will result in your body being parallel to the ground.

The Drive Phase (0m-20m)

This is the phase where you build upon the force that was applied during the start. Here you are to continue to keep your head and upper body down and maintain the form that you had at the start. One of the worst things that could happen is for the athlete to slow down or try to save their energy to use it later in the 100 meters. It is important that you teach the athlete to continue to drive through. Athletes do not want to place themselves in a position to have to struggle later in the race.

Acceleration (initial & full): (20m-45m)

In coaching we believe that this is the second most important phase. If the force from the start and drive phases are applied properly, then this phase will go according to plan. This is the phase where the athlete is getting ready to reach his or her maximum speed. After maintaining the drive phase successfully your whole body begins to slowly rise tall. Your stride becomes extended, your arms are pumping, and your hands are relaxed. The downfall of this phase is if you relax too much or back off of your speed, this could cause the athlete to injure him or herself. Learning the proper technique of this phase will be very successful for you.

Maximum Speed (45m-60m)

This phase speaks for itself; during this particular area on the track you will be hitting your top speed as an athlete. Your body will be high and tall and will be on the balls of your feet. Your stride and length will have increased since you are at top speed and your body has changed positions. Your hands are still relaxed, at this time you should be running very smooth and very fast.

Maintaining Speed (60m-100m)

After you have successfully completed the other 4 phases you are now coming to the phase that is vital and very important. During this phase you will find yourself running at top speed, only if you have completed the other phases correctly. You should still be relaxed, and you should still use the proper technique that you applied earlier. In this phase it is too late to drive or accelerate nor should you slow down. You must maintain the proper posture and mechanics during this phase. Not focusing on running this phase properly could result into losing the race or resulting in injury.

The Finish

Once you have completed every phase correctly you have seen great results down the track and you are now approaching the finish line. You want to keep that same intensity that you had when you started all the way to the finish line. When coming to the finish line you want to lean your upper torso across the line. Never slow down at the line; never get in the habit of doing that. You should run all the way through the finish line and end up on the top of the curve. With your focus you have achieved what you have desired to and that is a victory. So remember to follow these phases and your finish line experience will be a very exciting one.

100 METER TRAINING

FOLLOWING A FULL proof training method is something pretty hard to do, because of how the season is structured. The training material that is available can be hard to implement because there are a lot of different training methods. These numerous methods can cause you to have to water down the workouts. One thing we found out was if you manage and organize your workouts. The following are sample workouts for different times of the year.

Fall Training (Base Period)

During this period you are mostly conditioning, weight training, and teaching drills that aid in helping the athlete develop the proper form and sprint mechanics. In this section we also introduce workouts that help develop their cardio, breathing techniques, and flexibility training. With that it is never a dull moment in practice because you are doing many different things that help the athletes' body become stronger and fit in many areas that are going to be used during the season.

While in the Fall Training Phase you can do a variety of workouts. Here are some examples that can make your team better.

Sample Workouts:

- Sprint drills
- Strength Training/ Weight room (at least 3 times a week)
- Core Work (Pilates, abs, core stability circuit, and aerobics)

- Sprint techniques (arm motion, stride length)
- Pool Workouts
- Resistance Workouts

During this phase you also want to improve on the fitness level of each athlete. In high school this phase is very vital because it cuts down on the time during the months that you should focus on speed development. Having your sprinter in shape early is a great step in the right direction. The athlete will be at a point that when the season begins they will not have to struggle to get in shape and they can perform a peak levels throughout their season.

In Season Training Phase

This phase is a very important one because this is where your main focus is in developing speed, conditioning the body for the task that is needed, and also getting the athlete mentally prepared. You must teach your athletes that this phase is to prepare the team for the County, District, Regional, & State meets which is the Championship time. And they will be focused and ready for those events if you get them to work hard in this phase.

Sample Workouts:

- Continue to perfect your Sprint Drills
- Continue Strength/ Weight room Training (at least 2 times a week)
- Continue to do core work
- Introduce Plyometrics and Bounding Techniques
- Speed Development: Sled Pulls, Parachutes, and other exercises that you have to implement
- Block Starts (Read Section: Block Starts)
- Acceleration Drills: 2-3 Sets
- 5 x 20, 4 x 30, 3 x 40, 3 x 30, 3 x 40, 2 x 50, 1x60, 5x30
- Stairs or bleachers: 8-12; 2-4 sets

Sample Week Workout:

Monday – This day would be considered Sprint/ Endurance day. The workout would consist of 1100 to 1600 meters in distance. The workouts should also be done at a timely manner so that the athlete has a chance to work on form and also sprint mechanics.

Tuesday – This day is normally set aside for race preparation the day before a meet. You would do a short sprint workout; also you would work on starting block, relays, and field events.

Wednesday – TRACK MEET

Thursday – The emphasis on this day is very vital, because it is a day after the meet and you want to save their legs and also help them restore their muscles back to life. We recommend the athletes jog 1 mile and then work in the weight room. We use this method of training myself and my athletes never had an injury, this is because their muscles were strong enough to endure a long season.

Friday – Speed Development Day. You can bring out the sled, parachutes, and other items that can assist you in developing the athletes speed. Work on their main event.

Saturday and Sunday – There are some invitationals on Saturday, but not many, so these are your rest days.

Championship Training Phase

This is the phase that most athletes are excited about because they get a chance to compete on a great level. You want to concentrate on techniques; you want to rest the athletes a little more (because of the rounds that they run during this time). This training phase is more technical because you are fine tuning and making little adjustments that could produce a champion.

200 METERS

THE 200 METERS race is where the sprinter uses speed, strength and endurance. In high school you find that many runners have different talents in running certain events. In sprint training you would split your runners up into one of two categories: Sprinter (100/200) or Middle Distance Sprints (200/400). You will have some athletes that have the ability to go from the 100m to the 200m.

You want to determine early what category your 200m athletes fall into. Whether they will be placed in the speed type: 100/200 or mid-distant: 200/400. You also want to determine what type of training methods you are going to use and these methods should be geared towards their strengths. Just like the 100 meters you want to develop a training program throughout the year so the runner can develop in their strengths and weakness.

We recommend that you divide your year into parts:

- Pre-Season
- In Season
- Championship Season

Pre-Season

During this time you should incorporate drills, sprint techniques and workouts geared towards strength and endurance. Give them workouts that they could use to learn how to use their stride and quickness in their race. The earlier that this is taught and practiced the more comfortable the runner becomes with the drills and techniques. You will see the different in the way they perform in the 200 meters. You also want to begin conditioning, weight training, plyometrics, and running hills. Any type of resistance training would be great during this time also.

We would recommend that you set up parts of your season in a way that can be very productive for the athlete. Pre-Season is very important because it is where you can get a lot of your teaching and techniques done. You want to also begin conditioning drills, weight training, and any type of workout that will improve the athletes' skills in this event.

Example Workouts:

6 x 100m Technique runs

8 x 200m	Time: (M) 28sec. (W) 34sec.	Rest: 5-6 minutes
4 x 350m	Time: (M) 49 sec. (W) 52.5 sec	Rest: 10 minutes
4 x 600m	Time: (M) 1:58 (W) 2:05	Rest: 10-13 minutes
10 x 50m	Technique runs	

3 x150m build ups

80m-100m-150m-200m-150m-100m-80m

15 min runs

♂ – (M) Male Runner   ♀ – (W) Female Runner

As the coach you can break the workouts up any way you please. You may want to add stadium stairs, hill running, plyometrics, etc. But, in this section of training make sure that the basic materials of technique prior to moving to the next phase of training. We encourage you to teach relaxation through all of the phases of training. It is very important that the athlete remembers to stay relaxed and focused throughout their particular race.

In-Season Training

It is very important in this phase to be able to analyze and correct mistakes, because during the early part of the season it is easier to detect any mishaps in the athletes' technique or mechanics. The workouts in this phase are geared towards a sprint rhythm and fast paced efforts. Once the athletes have run you can see exactly what they would need to work on. Make sure that you keep a chart to track the times and keep a goal on the chart so you can make progressions throughout the season.

Example Workouts:

3 x 150m Build-ups

6 x 200m	Time: (M) 25 sec. (W) 29 sec. Rest: 2-3 minutes
4x 40m	(Fast paced Drill) Rest: 30 sec.
2 x 250m	Time: (M) 29 (W) 33 sec. Rest: 3-5 minutes
2 x 450m	Time: (M) 1:20 (W) 1:30 Rest: 8-10 minutes

♂ – (M) Male Runner   ♀ – (W) Female Runner

You also want to work on starts on the curve. You can work on the first 30 meters and move up by distance. This would ensure the success of the athlete while learning how to have a strategy for the 200 meters. Throughout these workouts you want the athlete to continue to be relaxed and also have a concentration on what the task is at hand.

We did not specify any days in this section because 100% of the time you would already recognized what sprint category your 200 meter runners are in. So, normally the workout would be geared toward 100m/200m or 200m/400m. Your workouts would be assigned according the categories they are in.

Championship Season

In this phase there will be a review time to make sure that the athlete is comfortable on everything that they have learned. And by this time the athlete should excel in this particular event. Make sure that the Start is correct along with the sprint mechanics and techniques. The athlete should also have race strategy remembered, you do not want the athlete to run someone else's race you want them to run their race and be prepared to achieve success.

400 METERS

IN HIGH SCHOOL a lot of runners try avoid running this particular race because it deals with having the speed of a sprinter and also having the endurance of a half-miler. We believe this is one of the most grueling of the 17 events that any track & field athlete chooses to run. Again you have to determine what type of 400 meter runner you have on your team. You have a sprinter type which 200/400 meter athlete, and then you have the half-miler which is 400/800 meter athlete.

You can determine what type of runner you have based upon their weaknesses and strengths. Once determined you can chose workouts accordingly to fit their strengths and weaknesses. The training and development will be much different because of the type of race the 400 meters is. The runner must have a great technical base in order to have success.

Your training will be broken up into 4 parts: Off-Season, Pre-Season Training, In-Season Training, and Championship Season Training. Truthfully, it is quite different because your 400 meter runner will need to have a great base of endurance to be effective in the training. So you will see the different of the parts of training and how intense and efficient it can be if you follow a training program.

Off-Season

This is a very unique training time because the high school athletes are now beginning school and they have about 5 months before the Track & Field season begins. The best way to get the endurance base that you need within those 5 months is to run **CROSS COUNTRY** yes we said it. We are firm believers in the effects that cross country has on a sprinter and a half-miler. It provides you with a great endurance base so when you start actual training in January you will be ahead of other athletes in your category. Based upon the type of athlete that you have you can adjust the length of time you spend on each part. Some athletes are more advanced than others.

Pre-Season

This part is very vital because the teaching process takes place. You will teach technique, race preparation, workouts, body mechanics, and the 400 meter strategy. We believe for the high school athlete everything should be broken down. So we are going to cover the type of workouts that you can provide for your athlete, which will ensure them great success.

The type of workouts that you have to cover is Speed Endurance, Tempo Endurance, Strength Endurance, and Speed. With speed endurance the runner takes in oxygen at a high rate. You can practice running distances are from 100m-600m. These are examples of workouts that you can use that would help your athlete learn how to recover faster.

Example Workouts:

- 5 x 100m   3-6 minutes rest
- 3 x 150m   3-6 minutes rest
- 4 x 200m   10 minutes rest
- 2 x 350m   10 minutes rest
- 1 x 450m   10 minutes rest

Tempo Endurance workouts help the recovery time to be short and also increase the intake of oxygen.

Example Workouts:

- 6 x 200m   2 minutes rest
- 3 x 300m   2 minutes rest
- 100-200-150-200-300-350   Walk the same distance for rest

Strength Endurance is a workout that involves activities that will proceed longer than 10 seconds. Doing any type of workout such as incline running, hill running, stadium steps, or any resistant training.

Example Workouts:

- 3 x 150m hill running
- 3 x 60 stadium steps
- 6 x 20 second jump rope

With those types of workouts you will put the athlete in the right direction for success in the 400 meters. Proper training will ensure that the athlete will know how to deal with the pressure and the stress of the 400 meters. It supplies their body with the competitive energy that it needs to achieve.

Speed is very important during the 400 meters and this type of workout will cover the distances of 40 meters to 150 meters. All speed workouts will be done at 100% on the curve or straight away. Rest will be determining upon the sets that are given in the workout.

Example Workouts:

- 3 x 40m starts
- 3 x 60m flying starts
- 4 x 100m sprints

In-Season Training

During this phase of the training there is still so much that you can be taught and learned, because now you are actually seeing the athlete run. You will know how to help the athlete develop the proper race strategy and you will know how to plan workouts properly. You will also be able to know exactly how to determine the goal times that you want to reach from the first meet until the last meet. The pace of the workout now changes to more of an up tempo workout because now the athletes' endurance should be intact.

Technique is very vital in this phase of training. As the season progresses, you will then need to rely on your technique and mechanics.

Sample In-Season Workouts:

Monday – Also called: Speed Endurance day. You workout distance would total between 1400m and 1600m. You work on a timely manner and you want to make sure you emphasize the rest period. Work on breathing and recovery time.

Tuesday – This is your Tempo/Strength Endurance day. You will put up tempo workout into play. Workouts such as: 5 x 200 and 6 x 50 stadium steps. Also, you have to remember that this is the day before a track meet. You could also work on starts and finishes.

Wednesday – TRACK MEET

Thursday – This would consider as your Event/Strength day. You could work on the parts of the 400m. Like the first 100m, second 200m, and the last 100m. You can also go to the weight room. With the weight room you will do your traditional workout for the first 20 to 25 minutes. Then, you can work on Explosive training such as Bounding, Squats, etc.

Friday – This is your Speed Day. The athlete can work on resistance and relays.

Saturday and Sunday – There are some invitationals on Saturday, but not many, so these are your rest days.

In-Season is it very important that you get the basic technique and training done in the Pre-Season, because the track season moves pretty fast and you don't want to be working on simple things that could have been done in the pre-season.

Championship Season

The challenge here is for you to keep the same type of schedule as in-Season, but the workouts are more upbeat and everything that you work on is fast paced. Your performance level will be determined according to how much the athlete takes in during their learning process. Most important is that the coach has made the proper adjustments and you will see the difference. Following a great plan can lead you to the State Championship, but it is up to you whether or not you endure the process.

SPRINTERS STRENGTH & CONDITIONING WORKOUT

Weight room

W E BELIEVE THAT the weight room is one of the most important and smartest things that a sprinter could indulge in. We have seen the benefits of placing weights within the athlete's workout, it can help them get stronger and aid in preventing any type of injury. You may ask yourself what type of workouts can be done that could strengthen the sprinter. Below will be some sample workouts that can be used or added to your weight program that you already have established.

There are different parts of the body that you can strengthen and we are going to share different workouts that are vital for developing a strong and competitive sprinter. There are many different workouts that can be used for the upper and lower body. You can break those workouts up into various days so you are able to strengthen the whole body and not only certain areas.

Before we get into the sample workouts we will go over safety in the weight room. Safety is one of most important aspects of lifting weights.

- You should be dressed properly: shorts, training pants, t-shirts, sneakers (gym shoes, and/or cross-trainers).
- Always have a partner with you to spot you whenever you lift any weights.

- Pay attention to what is going on around you, because you do not want to get hurt or hurt anyone else.
- Always come to work hard and be productive when you are working out.

Those are just a few things that could help make your weight room experience successful. As a coach you have to remember to lay down these rules early. Waiting may cause something bad to happen to an athlete while weight training.

Sample Workout:

We are going to cover the upper body first. There are many exercises that you can do that could help strengthen your muscles to perform well on the track.

Lower Body:

You can determine the sets and amount of reps that you would assign to each various exercises.

- Squats (Regular, Overhead, Seated, Split Squats)
- Cleans
- Leg Curls
- Leg Press
- Calf Raises (Standing or Seated)
- Toes Raises

Upper Body (Areas of Concentration: Shoulders, Back, and Triceps):

- Shrugs
- Triceps
- DB Bench Fly
- Dumbbell Shoulder Press
- Lat Pulls / Pull ups
- Dumbbell Row
- Overhead Press
- Dips
- Pushups (Wide, Diamond)

Upper Body (Areas of Concentration: Chest, Arms, and Bicep):

- Bench Press (Regular, Incline, Decline)
- Bicep
- Curls (Single, Straight Bar)
- Bench Fly

These are sample weight room exercises that can be done to improve the athletes' strength for Track & Field. You can determine the reps and sets to be done on the various days you set them on. You never want to work two consecutive days on the chest area you must give the chest area muscles time to recover.

Core Training

For the Track & Field athlete the core is one of the most important components. No matter whether you are a runner, jumper, or a thrower the core will be involved in whatever activity you choose. If you strengthen your core you will be able to run faster, jumper higher, and throw further. Core strength will give you greater mobility, improve your balance and stability, and improve your athletic performance on the track.

Sample Core Exercises:

- **Bridge feet extended**

Setup position
Position yourself flat on the floor with your hands flat facing down on both sides. Pull your feet toward your buttock with your feet flat on the ground all while tighten your abdominal muscles.

Movement
Press through your heels and raise your hips to align with your knee. Remember your head and shoulders should stay on the ground. You hold these drills for at least 15-20 seconds.

- **Bridge + Leg Extension**

Setup

This would be exactly like the Bridge Feet Extension.

Movement

While focusing on contracting your gluteal muscles, press through your heels while raising your hips. While positioning your heels directly below your knees, straighten one leg while keeping your knees aligned. Hold this position for 10-20 seconds.

• **Prone Bridge**

Setup

Getting on the floor with your legs fully extended, support yourself between your feet and forearms. Keep your elbows close to your sides and directly below the shoulders.

Movement

Keeping your tummy tight hold this position for 10-25 seconds. Do not let your hips drop.

- **Prone Bridge + Leg Lift**

Setup
Getting on the floor with your legs fully extended, support yourself between your feet and forearms. Keep your elbows close to your sides and directly below the shoulders.

Movement
Keeping your tummy tight, lift one leg several inches off the floor. Keep the big toe and upper part of foot pulled backwards. Hold this position for 10-25 seconds.

- **Side Bridge**

Setup
Positioned on your left side, with your right leg on top of the left, have the upper part of your foot pulled towards you. Hold this position for 10-25 seconds while having your right shoulder aligned with the left shoulder.

Movement
Keeping the tummy tight, raise your hips off of the floor, hold this position for 10-25 seconds.

- **Side Bridge + Hip Flexion**

Setup
Positioned on your left side, with your right leg on top of the left, have the upper part of your foot pulled towards you.

Movement
Using the same movement as the side bridge, flex the top hip and bring your knee parallel with your hips. Hold this position for 10-25 seconds.

- ## Side Bridge + Leg Abduction

Setup
Positioned on your left side, with your right leg on top of the left, have the upper part of your foot pulled towards you.

Movement
Using the same movement as the side bridge, flex the top hip and bringing the knees parallel with the hips. With the shin angled backwards and the big toe and upper part of your foot pulled backwards, hold this position for 10-25 seconds.

- **Hip Ups**

Setup

Lying flat on the floor, have your legs fully extended and your arms flat on your sides. Keep your tummy tight while pulling your big toe and upper part of your foot back towards you.

Movement

Press your heels into the ground. While holding this position for 10-25 seconds support your body weight on your heels, upper back and your shoulders.

- **Pelvic Thrusts**

Setup

Lie on the ground with your legs 90 degrees upward.

Movement

Slowly lift your hips off of the ground upwards. For 3 sets of 15-20 repetitions continue lifting and lowering your hips.

- **Russian Twists**

Setup

Sitting on the floor with hips and knees flexed 90 degrees while holding dumbbells or a medicine ball.

Movement

Swing from right to left while keeping your hips from rotating with the shoulders.

- **Dumbbell Lunges w/ crossover**

Setup
Stand with feet hip wide apart. Hold your dumbbells out in the front of your body.

Movement
Step forward 2-3 feet creating a 90 degree angle. To keep from causing injury, do not allow your front knee to extend past the big toe. Swing the dumbbells across your body towards your hips.

You can also use medicine balls, balance boards, etc. While strengthening the core you will be able to perform at a higher level in sprinting. You will see a major difference in how you workout, and perform due to the development of your core. In running track your core is one of the top 3 things to strengthen and work on. Core training is key in your ability to gain speed and improve your ability to be conditioned for more advance workouts.

Flexibility Training

Flexibility training increase joint motion, releases the tightness of various muscles, improves mobility and it also relaxes the muscles and joints. The high school students' muscles and body is changing everyday so flexibility is important. There are many types of flexibility training but we are going to cover the 2 that we think are very important:

1. Dynamic Stretching
2. Static Stretching

Dynamic Stretching is useful anytime before you run in a competition and it reduces muscle tightness before running.

Sample Dynamic Stretches:

- **Arm Swings**

    Standing tall, feet should be shoulder width apart, and slightly bend your knees. Your back should be straight. Arms are out to your side away from your body and you swing them forward, down, and backward. (10 to 12 repetitions)

- **Side Bends**

    Stand tall with back straight, feet just slightly outside of your shoulder width, knees will be slightly bent, with your hands resting on your hips. Bend smoothly first to one side and than to the other side, not leaning backwards or forwards. (Repeat 15 to 20 times).

- **Trunk Rotations**

  Stand tall with your feet shoulder width apart bending your arms toward your shoulders (or you can place them on your hips). Rotate your trunk to the right and then to the left. Remember to keep your legs and back straight at all times doing this drill.

- **Full Back Stretch**

  Lie flat on your stomach with your arm equal to your shoulders and you will use your elbow to raise your upper body until your back is curved in the form of a 'C'.

- **Abdominal Stretch**

  Lie down on the floor with your head and shoulders on the floor, bending your knees turn and place them on the floor extending your are to right side of your body drop your knees to the left side of your body and you must form a letter 'Z'. (Hold this for 10 to 15 sec.)

- **Hamstring/ Butt**

  Lie down with your back on the ground and lift one leg up while holding your knee into your body until you can feel the stretch.

- **Groin Stretch**

  Sit with your lower back straight with the soles of your feet touching. Use your elbows to push your knees to the ground. Leaning forward make this more difficult.

- **Alternate Toe Touches**

  Stand tall with your back straight you feet can be 2 feet apart; place your arms by your side. Remember to keep your arms straight, bend forward and twist your body. You want to touch your right toe with your left hand. Repeat those steps with the opposite hand.

- **Leg Swings**

    Extension / Flexion – Stand sideways to a wall, you would putting weight on your right leg and your left hand on the wall for balance and swing your leg forward and backward (8 to 10 repetitions on each leg).

    Abduction/ Cross-Body Flexion – Slightly lean forward with both hands on the wall and your weight on your right leg, swing your left leg in front of your body, your toes should be pointed upwards as your foot reaches the highest point, and swing your leg back down until it reaches it's final point (8 to 10 repetitions on each leg).

Static stretching is usually done when the body is fully warmed. Static stretching is also useful anytime there is tightness or discomfort.

Sample Static Stretches: Upper Body:

- **Shoulder & Chest**

    Chest Stretch – Feet should be shoulder length apart, stand tall with knees slightly bent, Hold out your arms to the side parallel with the ground and the palms of your hand facing forward stretching the arms back far as you can while doing this you should feel the stretch in your chest.

    Shoulder Stretch – Stand tall, feet should be shoulder width apart, knees slightly bent, your left arm should be parallel with the ground across the front of your chest, bend the right arm up and use the right forearm to ease the left arm closer to you. (Repeat with the opposite arm)

- **Triceps Stretch**

    Place both arms overhead and pull behind your elbow and you should feel you hand slide down to the middle of your back.

Sample Static Stretches: Lower Body

- **Glute Stretch**

  Lie flat on your back with your head and shoulders flat on the floor, you will bend your left knee and keep your right leg straight out in front of you. Raise the right leg that is straight above the left knee that is bent and reach through and grab the left leg the is bent and pull up towards your chest.

- **Adductor**

  Stand tall with your feet should be two shoulder widths apart, bend your left leg and lower body, always keep your back straight, and you will feel the stretch in the right adductor. (Repeat with opposite leg)

- **Hamstring Stretch**

  Sitting – You will sit on the ground with both legs straight out in front of you, bend the right leg and place your foot beside the knee of the left leg, allow the leg to be relaxed at this point, you will bend forward keeping the back straight. (Repeat with opposite leg)

  Standing – Having your legs straight and you go down with your upper body with your hands reaching for the floor.

- **Quadriceps Stretch**

  Lie face down on the floor, pressing your hips to the floor and bring your right foot up towards your buttock, take and hold your right foot with your right hand and pull slowly towards your buttock. (Repeat with your left leg)

- **Standing Calf**

  Stand tall with one leg in front of the other, place your hands flat and at shoulder height on a wall, place your leg back away from the wall keeping it straight and press your heel against the floor.

Plyometrics

Plyometric exercises improve explosion, power, and strength. This can also help improve your speed, your ability, and increase the power in your muscles. This is also used to help improve your core and strengthen your lower and upper body.

Lower Body:

- Squat Jumps
- Jump to box
- Lateral Jump to Box
- Lateral Box Push Offs
- Lateral Hurdles Jumps
- Single Leg Lateral Hops
- Split Squat Jumps
- Depth Jumps
- Bounding

Upper Body:

- Overhead Throws
- Side Throws
- Over Back Toss
- Slams
- Explosive Start Throws
- Single Arm Overhead Throws
- Squat Throws
- Tuck Jumps (Single leg)

You can do these exercises with a medicine ball and with the proper clothing on.

Pool Workouts

There are many advantages to incorporating pool workouts into your track program. Water workouts can work in many different ways. For example, it can help to improve the mobility of the runner, helps improves form and technique, and most important it is an aid into decreasing injury to keep your legs and muscles fresh. There are many types of water workouts that you can do to relax and to keep your athletes from being stressed throughout the track season. The main key is that your athlete will get a total body workout at one time which is the best type of training for strength.

Resistance Training

This is the type of training that some athletes love but often dislike the hard work that it takes to complete this type of training. With this type of training it can help improve components of speed, stride length, balance, foot speed, and it can increase jumping strength. In this type of training you can use Parachutes, Sleds, Over Speed Trainers, Resistance bands, etc. There is a lot of equipment that you could use in this particular training phase. You also want to be very careful that you do not do too much because the athlete could result into injury. Come up with a training regimen that would be great for developing that athlete's strength in this area.

THE MODEL ATHLETE NUTRITION PLAN

O NE OF THE most important aspect of Track & Field but not covered is how nutrition is one of the primary areas that could increase your life and most of all your performance in Track & Field. To reach your full potential as a runner you must be disciplined in your events and your nutrition. This is often a neglected area when it comes to high school track & field. For many runners, nutrition is made difficult due to the inability of supervision by a coach and mainly parents. In order to assess your athlete's sports nutrition level, you must ask the following questions:

- Do you know how the right nutrients can fuel your body and enhance your performance?
- Do you find obstacles in maintaining a good nutrition plan?
- Do you have a wide variety in your diet or do you eat the same foods consistently?
- Do you eat breakfast and lunch daily?
- Do you eat at least 1 vegetable per day?
- Do you eat at least 1 fruit per day?
- Do you consume foods from all food groups daily?
- Do you drink enough water to stay hydrated?

There are no secrets that as a young athlete having a well balanced nutrition plan can help fuel your body to become a better athlete. You must be disciplined and consider your overall nutrition when eating meals and snacks. There are no well thought out diets that will result in a complete nutritional plan that will work for all track runners. A well thought out nutritional plan throughout your track season will result in a commitment to building strong and energized track athletes.

The Basic Six Nutrients

Basic six nutrients of foods eaten:

1. Carbohydrates
2. Fats
3. Proteins
4. Vitamins
5. Minerals
6. Water

Carbohydrates

Carbohydrates are you greatest source of energy. They are the best healthy food that one can consume. Carbohydrates are the jet fuels of food. Sixty percent of your daily calorie intake should come from this basic nutrient. Great source of carbohydrates include bread, grains, cereals, pastas, fruits, and vegetables.

Top High-Carbohydrate Foods

The following are a must for your balanced diet:

- 100% whole grain bread
- Brown or whole grain rice
- Potatoes and sweet potatoes
- Dried beans and peas
- Whole grain cereals
- Skim or low-fat milk or soy milk
- Fresh fruits
- Fresh Vegetables
- 100% fruit and vegetable juice
- Whole grain pasta
- Yogurt or soy yogurt

- Whole grain pancakes and waffles
- High-energy sports bars
- Sports drinks
- Granola bars and cereal bars

Fats

Fat is a necessary part of every balanced diet. Fat takes a great deal of time for the body to convert into a usable source of energy. Excess amounts of fat are stored as body fat to be broken down at a later time if needed for energy. There are two types of fat, saturated and unsaturated. Saturated fats include animal fats which is damaging when too much is consumed. Common sources of saturated fat include butter, margarine, cream, salad dressing, cheese, shortening, whole milk, fried foods, chocolate, and pastries. Unsaturated fats are less harmful. Examples include corn oil, olive oil, and peanut oil.

Vitamins

Vitamins are chemicals that sustain life. They serve as metabolic catalysts that regulate all chemical reactions in the body. Many people take vitamins to give them energy. Vitamins do not provide energy. Food provides you with energy . . . not vitamins. A balanced diet will provide you with more than the minimum daily requirements for vitamins. The following table outlines the recommended daily intake for key vitamins for health and performance as well as the level not to exceed for each vitamin:

Vitamin	Recommended Daily Intake	Do Not Exceed
Biotin	30 mcg	Not Determined
Choline	550 mg	3,500 mg
Folate	400 mcg	1,000 mcg
Niacin	16 mg	35 mg
Pantothenic Acid	5 mg	Not Determined
Riboflavin (B2)	1.3 mg	Not Determined
Thiamin (B1)	1.2 mg	Not Determined
Vitamin A	900 mcg	3,000 mcg
Vitamin B16	1.3 mg	100 mg
Cobalamin (B12)	2.4 mcg	Not Determined
Vitamin C	90 mg	2,000 mg
Vitamin D	5 mcg	50 mcg
Vitamin E	15 mg	1,000 mg
Vitamin K	120 mcg	Not Determined

Minerals

Minerals form structures in the body. Bones, for example, are formed with the help of calcium. A balanced diet provides you with all the minerals you need. The following table outlines the recommended daily intake and upper limit for key minerals:

Mineral	Recommended Daily Intake	Do Not Exceed
Calcium	1,000 mg	2,500 mg
Chromium	35 mcg	Not Determined
Copper	900 mcg	10,000 mcg (10 mg)
Fluoride	4 mg	10 mg
Iodine	150 mct	1,100 mcg (1.1 mg)
Iron	8 mg	45 mg
Magnesium	400 mg	350 mg*
Manganese	2.3 mg	11 mg
Molybdenum	45 mcg	2,000 mcg (2 mg)
Nickel	Not Determined	1.0 mg
Phosphorus	700 mcg	4,000 mg
Selenium	55 mcg	400 mcg
Zinc	11 mg	40 mg

Water

Keeping your body hydrated is one of the most important keys to your athletic success as well as your overall health and fitness. The majority of our body is composed of water, and all the systems in our body are dependent upon water. Premature fatigue during a track meet and poor recovery can be the result of not drinking enough water each day. Once you begin to become dehydrated your performance can begin to decrease. Dehydration of your body weight can cause a decrease in performance. You want to begin any practice, workout, or track meet in an already hydrated state. It is very helpful to keep water or another non-caffeinated beverage with you throughout the day.

Use the following tips to help you maintain your daily hydration base:

- **Drink your ounces everyday:** You should consume at least 64 fluid ounces of water regardless of activity level. The more you weight the greater your fluid needs are
- **Keep your hydration base:** In anticipation of dehydration aim to consume 20 oz of water prior to practice or a track meet and 8 oz of water every 15 minutes throughout that meet or practice

- **Perspiration is a good thing:** When you are hot the body will sweat in order to cool down the blood.
- **Sodium is a must:** Runners that are prone to cramping should be sure to consume greater amounts of sodium prior to exercising and during periods of recovery. Sports drinks containing sodium as well as salty snacks (i.e. pretzels) can be helpful in doing this
- **Don't use thirst as an indicator:** If you are thirsty you are already dehydrated and the water that you intake will have little effect on your current state. As a result it is important that you follow your suggested fluid intake on a daily basis and don't base your fluid intake on thirst.

Note: The information in the section are facts from The United States Department of Agriculture, www.usda.gov and www.healthierus.gov the information provided is an effort to improve the health and wellness community in youth sports.

CONCLUSION

AS COACHES WE believe you should have a game plan for your athletes already set up. You the coach should be able to evaluate the runners on their progression made from the previous to the current season. For example, you should be able to have on record the average times ran in the previous season to compare to the current season. We believe in setting goals for your athletes because it gives them the insight and focus to train hard.

As a coach, you must be excited and enthusiastic about coaching. You should also expand your knowledge of training methods for your high school athlete. Upon doing so this will allow the athletes to have a chance to compete on a higher level of competition. This book was written by high school coaches for the high school coach and athlete. We hope that this book is informative and can be used as a tool to enhance your training methods as a coach and your determination as an athlete.

This is just the introductory book to the Fundamentals Series. Please look forward to the future publications of:

- The Fundamentals of Middle Distance
- The Fundamentals of Long Distance
- The Fundamentals of Field Events
- DVD Series of:

    o 100 Meters
    o 200 Meters
    o 400 Meters
    o 110/300 Meter Hurdles

- Jumps
- Throws
- Sprint Drills / Sprint Techniques
- Relays (4X100 and 4X400)
- Block Starts

TRAINING
WORKSHEETS

PLYOMETRIC TRAINING WORKSHEET

Warm-up Exercise:

Specific Technique Drills:

Sprint / Acceleration Drills:
____x10 meters ____x20 meters ____x30 meters ____x40 meters ____x50 meters

PLYOMETRIC EXCERCISES

Training Goals: you can focus on many different objectives in this exercise: Endurance, Strength, Power, Speed, Core, and General Training

Cool Down Period 10-- 12 minutes: laps and specific Stretches

DAILY TRAINING SESSION WORKSHEET

Date	Day	Week (1-52)	Period (Pre-Season, Season, Championship)

Warm-up Laps:

Specific Warm up/ Active Drill:

Specific Technique:

Acceleration sprints: example 4x10 meters, 4x20 meters

____x10 meters ____x20 meters ____x30 meters ____x40 meters ____x50 meters

Training Goals: (1) Endurance, (2) Strength, (3) Speed, (4) Agility, (5) Plyometrics, (6) Core, (7) Resistance Training, (8) General Workout

Workout:

Warm down: 7-12 minutes. Use time for specific warm down laps and also stretches:

WARM-UP, STRETCHING, & COOL DOWN WORKSHEET

Warm up drill:

Warm Exercises:	Specific Warm-up Drills:

Cool Down:

Cool down Exercises:

Specific Stretches for the cool down period:

Weekly Runners Strength/Conditioning Workout

Week: _____

Exercise	Monday	Tuesday	Wednesday	Thursday	Friday

Week: _____

Exercise	Monday	Tuesday	Wednesday	Thursday	Friday

Week: _____

Exercise	Monday	Tuesday	Wednesday	Thursday	Friday

Notes:

ABOUT THE AUTHOR'S

Eugene Shane Lee – is the Head Lady's Track & Field Coach at Hallandale High School located in Hallandale Beach, FL. He has been teaching and educating Track & Field athletes for 12 years and has also helped to develop athletes to win on the High School and College level. During a noteworthy career he helped coach Fort Lauderdale High School Boys & Girls Track & Field Teams to win 4 BCAA County Championships, 2 District Titles, 4 Regional Titles, and 1 State Championship. Coach Lee has helped produced many State Qualifiers in the 100m, 200m, Long & Triple Jumps, 4x100m and 4x400 relays. He is a member of The United States Track & Field Association, National Federal of State High School Associations for Track & Field/ Cross Country and also a Certified Personal Trainer. Coach Lee resides in Nashville, TN, but coaches in Florida; he is married to Andrea Girton-Lee.

To Contact Coach Eugene Shane Lee via email: e.shaneleecompany@consultant.com

Jeremiah Whitfield – is the Assistant Lady's Track & Field Coach at Hallandale High School located in Hallandale Beach, FL. He has been coaching and teaching Track & Field for 12 years while also helping athletes on the High School and College level. During the success of his career he assisted in coaching the Fort Lauderdale High School Boys & Girls Track & Field Teams to win 4 BCAA County Championships, 2 District Titles, 4 Regional Titles, and 1 State Championship. Individually he coaches a 4x800m relay team that won a State Championship which was ranked in the top 5 in the Country for 4x800 relay teams. Coach Whitfield has success in coaching individuals in the 400m, 800m, 1500, and the 2-mile races. Coach Whitfield resides in Fort Lauderdale, FL; he is married to Autumn Erica Whitfield and has 2 daughters.

To contact Coach Jeremiah Whitfield via email: jeremiahwhitfield@yahoo.com

Made in the USA
San Bernardino, CA
31 January 2017